How To Stop Enabling Your Adult Children

Practical steps to use boundaries and get your power back as you stop enabling

Introduction

This is the first step to getting your power back and feeling in control of your life and decisions again. There is a lot of great help out there in this area of enabling adult children. The aim of this book is to give you a very practical and accessible start to the process.

The key to change is understanding the mis-beliefs that are creating the current situation, and then having the practical 'How To's' that will empower you to challenge those mis-beliefs. As they are challenged we put in place new boundaries and strategies to stop enabling, and change can then occur. For someone who is stuck in the perpetual cycle of enabling and rescuing, this is an amazingly freeing process. You will feel empowered as you get your life back!

Understanding and implementing your new boundaries will be a gradual process. It will take time to feel that saying 'no' is not cruel. However, this is essential in order for your adult child to individuate and to take responsibility for themselves. You must stop rescuing them from consequences!

As your adult child individuates, it will be possible to lay a foundation for a new relationship with them that is more fulfilling and equal as you both take on the role of adult. Discover the wealth of shared experience that exists in sharing a mature and empathetic relationship with your adult child, instead of continually replaying the roles of parent / child for the rest of your life.

Welcome to this very practical introduction to understanding why you are enabling your adult children, and how you can be empowered to stop.

Melody Devonish

Table of Contents

Chapter 1 – Understanding the Enabler or Rescuer

As a new father or a mother, it is impossible to think of the day when this precious little bundle of joy would be old enough to think and act, let alone old enough not to need your assistance anymore. Every new parent is awed by the fact that the little baby they hold in their arms, a little person who is not yet capable of feeding on its own and who needs to be burped, cleaned, bathed and kept warm, will one day be old enough to know its' own mind.

Even when they are toddlers and infants, afraid of their own shadow and everything else in this big, scary world – it's 'mummy' and 'daddy' that they run to for comfort. "Mom, I'm hungry!" "Mom, I need you!" "Dad, I'm scared!" "Help me, mommy!" "Dad, help me get the Boogeyman out of my room!". These precious cries change in theme as they enter puberty. However, even then, it is you that they turn to with the words 'help' and 'need'. Although they would often never admit it, children need parents even more during those times.

So, when do our children really grow up? When exactly do they stop being children and become a citizen of this world? When they are legally an adult, or when they're old enough to vote? When they leave for college, leaving an empty room behind them that slowly gathers dust, only to be returned to during the holidays? When they get a job and move to another city, and you only get to see them through Skype or during Christmas? Or, is it when they get married and have a family of their own?

So, when is it exactly that they stop being your daughter or your son? When do you stop being a parent?

The answer perhaps is – never! You can never stop being a parent, no matter what, not even for a second. Even if your son or daughter is grown up and has grandchildren of their own, they are still your children. However as they grow up, it is ideal for your relationship if they can individuate and you can all re-define your relationships as adults. Although you are still the parent/child, you no longer treat each other (or think of each other) in the way that you did when the child was 16 years old.

This doesn't mean that you are no longer their parent. You are the parent when you snap the first photo of them learning to walk, when their hearts get broken the first time in high school, when they are confused about which major to choose in college, or when they are trying to decide their career. You are the parent when they bring 'the one' home to meet you, and when they are themselves coping with a new baby in their lives. Through thick and thin in their lives, between friends, dates and great loves, you are the parents.

However children leave home, and for the first time in years the nest is empty. This is the first time when all the children have completely left home - either to college, for work, or to their marital homes.

At least this is what ideally happens. Sometimes it doesn't happen, for various reasons, some more valid than others. If this break doesn't happen because of enabling, then your relationship with your child may have slipped into a place that is unhealthy for both of you. We will cover this topic soon.

However, ideally your children find their way out into the big wide world, and they leave your home. This is an incredibly important time for you and your partner. This is the time that couples can be completely alone with each other again. Even if your children mean the whole world to you, you should never forget that you are an individual first, and also a couple. Parents tend to lose themselves completely in their children, forgetting their true selves and their relationships with each other while caring for children.

Yes, this is a time to be sad when the children are grown up and don't need you anymore. However it is also the time to rejoice, to catch up with your partner and rekindle the old fire.

This is the time to travel the world, let romance and sex into your lives once more and enjoy your time together.

However, that is not always the case. We all know of some not-so-normal cases where the children, even after they are working adults, and sometimes even married – are keen to live with their parents, at their parent's home. And by the not-normal cases, we mean when the children are able-bodied, healthy and capable of living on their own. In some situations and cultures it is completely healthy and balanced for this to happen. However this book applies to those situations when it is not healthy for those involved, and can actually become incredibly destructive.

In some cases, the children may be living apart in their own houses or apartments, but may still be dependent on the parents for financial support, help with chores, advice, food and medical attention.

In more extreme situations parents are expected to take responsibility for an adult childs' drug addiction, or to continually bail them out from run-ins with the law. An adult child may cause their parents' extreme debt and financial instability as they make continuously bad choices and expect their parents to rescue them...and the parents do! Over and over again. There are also many cases of adult children abdicating responsibility of their own children to the grandparents. This is not simply baby-sitting; it is a true abandonment and handing-over of their children on a regular basis. These situations often occur without warning and are truly manipulative, as there are grandchildren involved who the grandparents deeply love.

In each of these cases, we have two parties: the adult children who are opting to live in their parent's houses and/or take advantage of them, and the parents who are either encouraging or not discouraging this behaviour. Let us call these parents the *enablers* or the *rescuers*.

HELPING SOMEONE OUT IS NOT ENABLING (OR

RESCUING). EVERYONE NEEDS HELP SOMETIMES AND
THAT'S OKAY. ENABLING IS DOING FOR SOMEONE ELSE
WHAT HE OR SHE CAN AND SHOULD BE DOING FOR
THEMSELVES.

Parents are rescuers at heart. Parents are programmed to
rescue their children from everything; from when they are
young and afraid of a barking dog, or a teenager afraid of a
failing grade, to when they are an adult afraid of a demotion of
getting fired at work. We as parents are always there to help
with any problem our children find themselves in.

Let's be frank with ourselves for a moment and ask, 'do my
children still need me to do the things I do for them?'. Yes,
when they were younger, parents have to do everything for
their children; because the children literally can't do anything.
But as they grow older and more responsible, children should
take up some of the chores around the house. This could be
the simplest of chores such as cleaning up after themselves,
tidying their toys and books, setting the table, or doing the
beds.

Letting your children learn to work and look after themselves
is the healthy choice. However, some parents make it a habit
to look after their children so much that the children become
completely incapable of being independent or looking after
themselves. They are the children who later on, after growing
up, never leave their parent's house but prefer to stay
financially and socially dependent on their parents.

There are various reasons a parent may start this habit of
looking after their children too much. However the point is
that it did start; that as the parents you began to enable your
child when they were young, and so they learnt to play the role
of the enabled child. You have both learnt your roles in this
relationship, and they need to change.

You may have felt cruel whenever you said **'no'** to your child,
and so you didn't say no. Consequently your child *never
learnt how to deal with disappointment.* Therefore they don't

know how to deal with it when you or someone else now tries to say no to them. Your child may be an adult now, but they still can't cope with disappointment, as they never learnt. *To them it is truly intolerable, and may even make them feel rejected.*

Saying no when it is the appropriate answer is obviously not rejection, however your adult child may need to be re-trained in this. You may have a weekend away all booked and paid for... and they ask you to baby-sit so they can go to a party. 'No' is obviously an acceptable answer; you already have plans and they probably have other people they can ask. However their reaction is certainly not reasonable. In fact it can reflect the reaction they had when you said they couldn't tear the pages of a book when they were six years old.

Let me guess, you gave in and let them tear the pages? That's why they expect you to give in now. They have been trained to expect you to enable them and give in.

Are you wondering how this happened? When did you become an enabler or a rescuer to your grown-up, adult children? Let's start from the beginning, shall we?

Chapter 2 – How the Enabling Cycle Continues and Grows

Congratulations! You have just had a new daughter or son, and you are feeling like two of the happiest people in the world, and rightly so. Becoming a parent is one of the most amazing things that can happen to a person, and the joy that a baby brings to a family is immeasurable.

But now begins the hard part. The baby needs to be breastfed and bottle-fed, cleaned and diapered, bathed and clothed, burped and lullaby-ed, and it is entirely the parents' responsibility.

If you think your responsibilities will lessen once the child is slightly older, you are sadly mistaken. As children begin to walk and run, it is the parents' job to run right behind them, protecting them from bumping their heads and picking them up when they fall.

When they finally reach school-going age, it the perfect time for you to get them started on simple chores around the house. However, kids this age have agendas of their own, and start to have their own priorities. Trying to make them do the simplest of tasks takes up a lot more time than to actually do the job yourself. Therefore, instead of asking them and teaching them, parents often end up simply completing the task themselves. And so the children, at a very early age, understand that if they manage to ignore a chore for a certain period of time, their parents will end up completing it, and they won't have to leave their games.

Thus, the seeds of entitlement are sown. This is dangerous territory for parents, as it is where the mind-set of your child is being developed. Mind-set is key here, as is it where behaviour stems from. The mind-set they are developing in these earlier stages will stick with them later.

As they continue growing, getting them to do chores around the house becomes even more difficult. They mature and they begin to grow a life outside the house, filled with new friends, sports and teen obsessions. If they have not been taught to take responsibility for themselves and their chores, then why would they interrupt their lives to do it? Many parents (after screaming, bribing, threatening and asking) resign and complete the tasks themselves. Young adults who are completely capable of doing a number of tasks on their own never do any of them, because they have their parents as a backup.

Requests can start to sound dangerously like orders; "Mom, why isn't the laundry done?" "Dad, is my lunch ready?", and yet they are completely capable of doing each and every one of these tasks themselves.

By this time, if the parents are weary of the fact that their children do absolutely nothing to help in the house, it is almost too late. These children have learned from a very young age that if they leave a task undone for some time, Mom and Dad are going to: a) ask them to do it, b) ask them again, c) scream at them once or twice to do it, and then, d) do it themselves. Easy way out!

And soon mummy and daddy will find that they are the only ones who are doing absolutely all the work in the house: the cooking, the cleaning, the laundry, the mowing, cleaning the children's rooms, making them breakfast, lunch and dinners, cleaning up after them, and everything else - while the children sit around watching TV and sipping lemonade.

When they are accepted to the college or university of their choice and are finally out of the house for good, things are going to change right? Quite unlikely! By this time, your children are so dependent on you that the requests/demands won't stop, even from a distance. This time, the queries will be of a different pattern: "Mom, did you pack my blue sweatshirt?" "Mom, you didn't pack my tennis shoes; I need them here!" "Mom, I think I left my mobile charger back at my room. Can you please have it sent to me?".

The demands from your maturing child may fall into the range of requests that are draining but in themselves harmless. Or they may fall into the category of more serious demands, as they continue to act in the entitled manner they are accustomed to, while still expecting to never have to suffer the consequences. In fact, it never OCCURS to them that they would have to suffer consequences, as they have never had to before. Why would that change now?

Your child is caught selling marijuana, and you do everything in your power to cover it up and help your poor misunderstood college student to 'get back to their studies'. Your son or daughter continually max out their credit card, buying more and more things that they 'need', and entertaining their new college friends on the weekend. But it would be cruel to let them suffer the consequences and just be broke for the rest of the month right? So you keep topping up the credit card, even when you and your partner really can't afford it. Even if you can afford it, by letting them continually break their work and avoid repercussions, you are simply re-affirming the message that consequences are for other people, not them. They can have this entitled attitude, because you will help them get away with it, and even support it.

After they graduate this won't stop. There is a chance that your graduate son or daughter would find it too hard to get an apartment by themselves in the city, and opt to live with you 'for the time being'. They are always tired from work, or from partying and still have no time to help you with the cooking or the cleaning. But can you please make them their favorite 'Mac and Cheese' this Sunday? "Can you please iron my good suit, Mom? I have a presentation this week!", and we are back to the beginning. "Mom, where's my strappy blue sandal?" "Have you seen this huge file I brought home last week?" "Can I borrow your tie, Dad? And your shoes? And the watch? I have an interview".

Do you see the pattern yet?

Poor you! You have always dreamed of a Europe trip with your partner, but now it seems quite impossible! Who would make Junior's dinner? How would he ever find clean clothes if you are not there to do the laundry? The house would be in shambles if you guys leave for a month! Who would clean? And dust, and vacuum? Certainly not Junior, he has no idea how to use the oven!

Your adult child's thinking has not changed since he/she was small and refused to do chores, or demanded the expensive birthday present that was never even used. *Their thinking is just the same, and the roles you are all playing haven't changed.*

So why would their behaviour change?

You may still be thinking, "It's just for a few more months! He will move out soon". Perhaps he will, but he will always be dependent on you and your partner, at least for a long time. Even if they do get an apartment for themselves, rest assured, there will still be piles of laundry dropped in, and they will themselves be dropping by several times during the week for dinner because they 'missed your cooking' (try 'didn't feel like cooking').

And that is still not the end. You and your partner will be the first choice when they need a babysitter, when they need a loan, when they need somebody to moan to, somebody to point their fingers at, and somebody to fall back on.

"There's this show that we have tickets for this Sunday, mom. We'll be dropping the kids at your place at 7.00."

"What do you mean you have plans with Uncle Eddy? Surely they are not that important? Why don't you un-invite him and do it again next week?"

"You know how the kids love spending time with you guys! They miss you so!"

Just a son or a daughter depending on their parents? Or, straight emotional blackmailing?

What is going on here that needs to change? WHY is this cycle happening?

It's all about mind-set. How we think creates our reality.

The Greek author Plutarch said:

"What we achieve inwardly will change outer reality."

This is so true; the mind is a powerful tool. The mind interprets and creates the reality we live in. This interpretation all stems from the beliefs that we hold. These beliefs may be good and helpful or they may be harmful, either way they will influence how we travel through life.

In the area of enabling, there are often some harmful beliefs about being cruel, or 'needing to be needed' that drive the enabler. If the enabling is being driven in this way then it is no longer a case of 'just stopping'. If you could just stop, you would. You know that enabling is bad for your child, and it obviously has negative repercussions in your life too.

So why can't you just stop?

Your logic knows that this is not working for you, and yet you continue repeating the same pattern over and over. The reason for this is your deep programming. This programming is sub-conscious, and 'over-rides' your conscious attempts to use will-power to change.

You think to yourself, "next time my son/daughter makes another completely unrealistic request of me ('borrowing' money / endless child-care etc), then I will simply say 'no'. I will say that we can't afford it, or that we aren't able to take time off work AGAIN to look after your children for a few weeks, or we simply don't have the time and energy to fly to another city to help you move house again".

However, when the phone call comes, and the discussion starts, things change. The guilt starts to flood in as your beloved son/daughter starts to 'explain'. Your logic may even be telling you that they are manipulating you, that even though there are elements of truth in their struggle, he/she is an adult and needs to take responsibility for his/her life. However, your deeper subconscious over-rides this spunky spark of logic, and the guilt prevails.

You will now do anything to avoid this feeling of guilt or cruelty that is clawing away at your insides. This feeling is tapping at the door, trying to come in, and you KNOW that you can't stand it. It's intolerable. So to avoid this feeling you say, "of course we can help you move...this one last time"...or, "yes you can borrow that money"...or, "you know that we love to baby-sit. Yes two or three weeks is a long time, but since you are in such a difficult situation...".

And magically that awful feeling evaporates. We don't have to confront that intolerable feeling that was tapping away, threatening to come in and upset us. The guilt departs. We may even feel a bit saintly in our victim-hood.

Do you see how this cycle will keep repeating itself? Not only is the adult child rescued from the consequences of life, but the resentment that the parents feel will only grow, as more and more unhealthy pressure is put on both their relationship with each other and with their adult children.

Cognitive Behavioural Therapy (CBT) calls this an Intolerable Feeling (Edelman, 2006).

This cycle can be challenged, and change can happen. It is a VERY empowering process. Getting your power back in your life, and feeling the freedom of being in control of your decisions is an amazingly freeing process. It does however take work, and it will be uncomfortable at first. After all, change is rarely easy.

However the alternative is that things stay the same, and if you wanted things to just stay the same I very much doubt that you would have bought this book.

Later in the book we will get further into the process of changing your enabling actions by adapting your thinking in this area, and learning how you can do this.

Chapter 3 – Dignified Assertiveness, Boundaries Are Your Friend!

Your children are one of the most important parts (if not the most important part) of your life. Parents would give their lives for their children without a second thought, and there is no one else in this world that a parent loves more than their own flesh and blood.

But that doesn't mean you have to spend your entire life picking after them and rescuing them from consequences. For your own sanity, and for their sake, your priority in life must be nurturing your children in such a way that they grow up to be confident, independent, beautiful human beings, and not just a bewildered, shriveling person who doesn't know what to do with him or her-self.

For your children's sake, you need to set some strict boundaries around yourselves. Whether you have adult children living with you, or your 40-year-old son is still completely dependent on you financially, there are a few boundaries that you as parents need to put in place and maintain.

If you reflect on your situation and realize that you are being taken advantage of, and you are enabling, then it is likely that the boundaries you have tried to put in place are being constantly over-run. If this is the case, then it is time to learn some **dignified assertiveness**.

Here are some boundaries that you can start with. These are very acceptable expectations to place on an adult child, and would ideally be already functioning in a parent/adult child relationship. Remember, these boundaries are NORMAL, HEALTHY and OKAY. You are not asking too much by requesting that these be respected.

Start acting like an adult

It is time to treat them as though you expect them to act like an adult. When your children have grown up, it is time that they start acting accordingly. If your son, the college graduate, is still living with you and showing no signs of applying for a job, but instead spends his days sleeping and playing video games, that is the time to set up a boundary. If your daughter is moving from one odd job to another, and expecting you to repeatedly take her in and financially support her without warning or negotiation, it is time to act up.

"You are old enough; you know better. You are a capable, intelligent human being with a bright future ahead of you. It is time for you to start settling down in life and chose a path. Be an adult; act your age."

This should be your stand: that they are old enough, they are adults; they should know better. Plenty of children refuse to grow up and become adults when they are so comfortably settled in their parent's lives. You have to remove them from their comfort zone so that they can take responsibility for themselves and start living their lives.

Keep your privacy

Whether your adult children are living with you, or whether they have separate accommodation, you are entitled to privacy and solitude. Although they are your children, they must respect your need for privacy. They cannot just drop by whenever they want and demand your complete attention. You and your partner may have plans of your own that don't concern your children.

Just because they are your children doesn't mean that they do not need to consider your plans. You are entitled to a phone call beforehand asking for permission so that they can visit.

If they are living separate, then it is often the case that they have a set of keys for your house for emergencies. However, having a set of keys does not mean that they can drop in unannounced and without knocking. If they know you are home and if it is not an emergency, they should wait at the door and use the doorbell to gain admittance.

Let them be financially independent

While it is okay to lend your son some money to buy a car or even give him a car as a present, whatever happens to the car is his and his responsibility alone. If he totals the car and needs to pay the victim of the accident, or if the car needs repair, you should not be the one who is paying.

An expensive designer dress for your college-graduate daughter on her birthday or Christmas is a one-time thing. If you can afford it, you should definitely go for it. But if she comes to you every time she sees a dress or a bag that she just loves, but she is out of her pocket money, it is not your responsibility to satisfy her whim. She is old enough to get a job, or to save up for what she needs.

If your adult child is repeatedly expecting you to pay their seemingly endless parking or speeding fines, this is not okay! It is fine to expect them to take responsibility.

If you go on providing a strong financial support at every turn of their life, they will never learn.

So, help your children out, but don't make it a regular event. Finance them for their first business idea, but don't let them expect help every time they are facing a loss. Putting a $20 bill in their hands when you know they are in a tight spot is fine, but don't make a habit of it; and most importantly, don't let them make a habit of it.

In an example of more extreme cases adult children will be expecting their parents to financially support a drug habit or gambling addiction. And the parents will do it! If you have all been trained enough in your enabling/enabler roles, you as the parents will simply not be able to say 'no'...even when you are supporting your childs' $500-a-week drug habit, and you know it!

Soon we will look into how this mind-set can be changed. However, first take hold of the assurance that it is okay and *right* to say no in this area of financial support. This change won't be easy, but it is absolutely necessary for all involved.

"Not under my roof"

Your children may have grown up to be adults, but while they are living under your roof, they have to follow your rules. This could mean doing their own laundry, helping out with the cleaning, and even cooking dinner for the family at least once a week. No matter how old they are, or what expenses of their own they may have, if they are under your roof they have to contribute to the expenditures of the house.

"You cannot be out till 2am at night, and then expect me to wait up with dinner!" "I'm sorry but it's unreasonable to think it's ok to spend your entire weekend out or playing on your PC, and not doing any of the chores" "The agreement is that you do the dishes twice a week, no matter what important assignment you have to work on!" "Not under my roof; that is unacceptable!"

If you find this kind of request impossible, and you feel like you're 'walking on eggshells' around your house, then it is time to do something! Repeated and calm dignified assertive statements and boundaries need to be put in place. These will not necessarily be received well by your adult child. But it is ESSENTIAL that you stick to your new boundaries, and keep repeating your stance in a calm and assured manner.

You have to be strict to some extent. If your children think they are entitled to live with you, do not let them live through you. They are old enough to take on their own responsibilities, even if it is under your roof.

Chapter 4 – The Importance of Individuation

Individuation is an essential part of our development process. It is the process of becoming aware of oneself, of becoming an individual and discovering the totality of Self. This is generally the process we go through as we're progressing into adulthood. Although individuation is an internal process, it is also encouraged or discouraged by external factors and messages. Constant enabling and over-the-top protection of a younger child can stunt their process to individuation when they are older.

The process of individuation generally has two aspects: independence and separation.

From the first moment that we learned to spoon-feed ourselves, to the moment we got our first job, our entire life is a journey to become an individual. We are learning to stop only being someone's son or daughter or sibling, and becoming our very own person.

As we grow we develop opinions: a favourite color, a favourite food, a favourite dessert, a favourite toy; these are entirely our own. These are the stepping-stones to becoming our own person; we are still integrally linked to, but also increasingly individual from, our parents and everyone else that we know.

It is important that children have this sense of individuation from a very early age. Children who have not learned to recognise themselves as independent human beings from their early childhood, have problems in thinking of themselves as individuals even when they are adults.

For the younger children, start early.

Help your children in their tasks, but more importantly, help them learn to help themselves.

Give them advice when they seek it, but don't expect them to abide by all of your wise counsel.

Teach them to do something, and then stand back to watch them try and fail, try and fail, and finally succeed at it.

Though their first burst of opinions may surprise you in the beginning, remember, they are growing up! They are individuals and they have their own lives ahead of them. Parents will not be there forever. There will be a time when they have to make their own decisions and trust themselves to make a wise choice.

For the older children, the concepts are somewhat similar. Just because they have become adults does not necessarily mean that they have managed to find magical solutions to every problem. There will still be problems in their career, their finances, their marital life and their parenting that will make them come to 'Mommy' and 'Daddy' for solutions. What do you do for them?

They are old enough to know right from wrong, and good from bad; but still they are asking for your help. You cannot just say, "No! Find your own solutions". But you also don't want to become 'Agony Aunt' every time they face a dilemma.

What you can do, is you can listen. Listen to them, try to understand, and when it comes to finding the solution, ask instead: "What do you want to do?" "What do you think needs to be done?" "How do you feel this should end?" "Is there anything that you have in mind for this trouble?".

Sometimes, a good question brings you halfway to the answer. To become an individual person, they will need to know their own minds. They will be surprised to see that they themselves had the answers, or could work them out, but didn't know how to start.

We are going to look at the two aspects of individuation: independence and separation.

Independence

The concept of independence is not hard to understand, and oftentimes is extremely enjoyable. When do our children really become independent? When they are of age, and when they leave the nest to pursue their own lives.

If you have taught your children well, as a parent, you should have no fear of your children's independence. You should have faith in them that they wouldn't do anything reckless or careless.

As for the adult child, freedom may finally mean being able to stay up as long as they want to, staying out as late as they wish to, living on junk food, or even not showering for days in a row. As obsolete as they sound, these are the steps of rebellion and behavior through which a person becomes an adult. These are the steps that a parent often needs to *not* comment on as the children work out for themselves how they want to do things in life.

Separation

The concept of separation too might be a little difficult for parents to understand, as is the concept of 'letting go'. Separation is a slow stage when parents and children begin to understand that they are not one person but two, and that they each have their own opinions and decisions in life.

This is actually a long process, starting from when a parent suddenly knows that she/he doesn't have to take the child to the supermarket anymore, or that they are capable of staying home safely by themselves. Or when the father can no longer lift his son on to his shoulders but the boy can walk beside him and match his strides. Or when parents do not have to read out loud and point to the pictures in a book, the child has already learned to read.

All the years of taking care of a child is actually a process of preparing them to be an individual so that they are ready to face the world on their own.

These are obviously the stages of individuation that would ideally happen with your adult children. However, in situations involving enabling by parents, this process is generally delayed or even completely avoided by the adult child.

Chapter 5 – 'It's Not Cruel to Say No!'
Changing Your Thinking (Cognitive Behavioural Therapy)

If, whenever you say no to your child, you feel cruel, inadequate, un-loving, or like you will do anything to keep the peace, then it's time to change your thinking.

Let's look at how we can change this mind-set.

The change has to start with you as you put up your boundaries and then calmly continue to insist that they be respected.

In chapter two we started looking at your deep programming, or *subconscious beliefs*, when Cognitive Behavioural Therapy (CBT) was introduced. Now we will look at how this approach can help you challenge your beliefs and start the process of change.

Change happens as we challenge those disruptive deep, subconscious beliefs that are wreaking havoc on our decision making process. You may not even be aware that they are there.

These deep *subconscious beliefs* feed our *conscious beliefs*. Our *conscious beliefs* feed our *self-talk*; what we say to ourselves, our internal monologue. For example, as you pick up that chocolate bar you say to yourself: "I deserve this", or "one won't really make a difference". Or as you walk into a job interview you're saying "I've got this, I'm ready", or "they won't like me; I never make a good first impression", or "what if I screw up, I can't handle that".

This *self-talk* directly creates your *emotions*. You feel anxious, confident, insecure, or fearful, and it all comes from what you say to yourself.

These feelings then directly impact your *behaviour*. Where do you look when you shake hands in a job interview? How does your posture differ if you're feeling either insecure or confident? Do you even GO to the job interview? Your *self-talk* and consequent *emotions* impact whether you go ahead and buy that chocolate bar.

The basic CBT approach is:

Subconscious beliefs feed our:

Conscious beliefs, which feed our:

Self-Talk, which create our:

Emotions, which drive our:

Behaviour

So if we can start to challenge some of those deeper beliefs it will lead to a change in our behaviour; instead of trying to do it on a behavioural level by will-power alone.

This same process is the one that creates the feelings of guilt or cruelty in the nightmarish cycle of enabling.

This also explains why just trying to change things at the behavioural level is generally a pointless mission. If those deep beliefs are constantly surfacing and creating intense emotions, then what chance can will-power alone have? You might last for a few weeks, even a bit longer, but those deep beliefs will win out.

Will-power definitely has its place, but it NEEDS to be backed up by a shift in thinking. It needs to be backed up by you challenging those deep beliefs, and CHANGING YOUR SELF-TALK. Once the deep beliefs are identified and you have started to challenge them, then your self-talk will change. As your self-talk changes, your emotions and then your behaviour will also subsequently shift, and you will gradually start the process of **getting your power back**.

However you need to have some very solid tools to enable you to challenge these beliefs. These beliefs that are causing you to constantly slide back into your old enabling ways will not just go quietly. They have been your 'old friends', and they will kick up a fuss. You will be uncomfortable. You will also have to be stubborn and hold on as you bring in this new empowering phase in your life.

There is a lot more information on CBT and the process of change out there, but hopefully this book will give you a very practical and useful introduction to it.

LIMBIC-LAG

This section is a brief introduction to the brain and how it responds to our attempts to change.

The limbic system is a part of our nervous system. Our brain has two parts: the *limbic* and the *neo-cortex*. The limbic system is our emotional brain. The neo-cortex relates to our ability to reason, and obviously develops slowly as we grow up. The neo-cortex deals with logic. Think about it, a new-born baby doesn't have the ability to reason, but they do start to develop this over the first five years of their lives. The limbic system is however working full-blast in a new-born baby.

The limbic system tags experiences with emotions. As a baby/small child we 'tag' and understand these experiences according to our emotional reaction to them.

When an experience is bad we avoid it, and when it's good we want more. We make these 'tags' when we are too young to know better. Obviously some of them are great, but I'm sure you can see how some un-helpful connections could be made; for example, 'it's dangerous to say no'. If you tagged a truly awful emotion to saying 'no' or placing boundaries, then it makes sense that you will avoid doing this at all costs later in life.

These 'tags' or conclusions can be re-trained and re-programmed through life experiences. However we can also encourage this re-programming process.

Changing your mind, or deciding to do something differently, doesn't have lasting effects if you don't combine it with re-programming your limbic system.

Limbic lag refers to the delay or 'lag' that there is as your brain catches up to a new way of doing things. It WILL catch up. However, this requires you to take over and teach it to catch up.

As you go through this re-programming you are creating new neural pathways.

A very practical example of this is when you have to drive on the other side of the road. You travel from England to France, or the USA to Australia, you rent a car, and suddenly you are driving on the other side of the road! At least, everyone else is, so you'd better be as well. Your logic knows this. You've had the brief from the rental company, and have had people teasing you about 'driving on the wrong side' for weeks.

It is COMPLETELY CORRECT for you to be driving on the wrong side of the road; in fact it would be very dangerous if you did otherwise.

Your logic knows this and is convinced of this new reality, however you limbic system hasn't quite caught up. It's not quite convinced yet, and your mind needs to act as an over-ride (and stay on the correct side of the road!) while your limbic system is taught a new way of behaving.

The first time you turn a corner, or go through an intersection your limbic system is SCREAMING at your body to get back on the correct side of the road. This is not just a little urge, this is a deep instinctual NEED to get off the wrong side of the road, or you are in danger.

The same thing happens when we first challenge those troublesome deep beliefs in life. It's not just a little urge to ignore the new way of thinking and maintain the status quo; it is a deep instinctual need to keep the status quo to keep safe.

This is why change is uncomfortable. You need to be fully convinced that it is necessary for you to stop enabling your adult child in order to have your mind over-ride your deep beliefs and limbic system. You need to be FULLY convinced of how incredibly harmful it is for both you and your adult child if things don't change. Because it is truly harmful; it is destructive to all of your relationships. As they are constantly rescued from consequences you are stopping them from becoming the responsible, contributing, full human they have the capacity to be.

All of this is why you need to be fully and completely convinced that change is needed. When you are convinced, then your new mind-set can challenge the old mind-set, and win. Just as you need to be FULLY convinced that you must stay on the correct side of the road in that new country. As you turn that corner and your limbic system is telling you to get to the other side of the road, your mind NEEDS to be ready and able to over-ride it. In this way it will keep you safe as you continue on your new way of behaving.

Your new behaviour is to drive on the other side of the road. As you continue to do it, it slowly becomes more natural. Your brain develops new pathways or 'grooves', and you no longer feel un-safe on this new side of the road. In fact, it becomes normal.

This is the same process we go through as we enact change in our lives.

SO HOW DO WE DO THIS?

Various authors, counselors and experts in the area of CBT, REBT and other counseling methods have different names for the process of challenging problem beliefs. To keep things simple we are going to call them insights, or coaches.

Basically these are simple and yet powerfully accurate things we say to ourselves to create new pathways or 'grooves' in our brain. This is not just 'positive thinking', or happy thoughts. These coaches that we use will literally re-program your way of thinking. They need to be both specific and accurate for them to work. When those challenging situations occur you need to hold onto them like a drowning person holds onto a life-saver.

These insights need to be in place before that phone call comes, or that visit happens. You need to be fully convinced of every word in these new coaches, and they need to be running through your head before you go into that challenging situation.

You know your adult daughter is coming over to ask you to co-sign for a loan for her new house, and you KNOW that you have to say no. Or your adult child again needs a babysitter for the weekend so they can go out and party. You know it would be the worst thing for your finances and/or your state of mind to say yes again. However, before she arrives you need to have these new coaches playing in your head, in order to challenge your old self-talk. As you dwell on these new insights, and you know that they are replacing your harmful subconscious beliefs, then new self-talk is created. It will be a battle, especially the first few times. However as time goes on, it will become more natural. As you regain your power through dignified assertiveness, you will be able to stick to those boundaries. The boundaries that your adult child used to knock over like a wall of match-sticks.

Now, when your adult son comes to you with another request to pay off his fines, or your daughter expects you to bail her out of prison again, you know what you will be repeating to yourself. You have something to fall back on; you have your life-saver already in place so you don't start flailing and 'drowning'. In the same way that can't learn to swim while you're drowning, you can't learn to change your thinking while you're in the middle of a situation that is causing you all sorts of horrendous emotions and reactions that you just want to avoid.

This is why it's so important to have this new programming in place before you go into that situation or conversation.

Be gentle on yourself; you won't get it perfect immediately. If your problem is that you feel cruel when you say no, then you have to expect that you will still feel cruel. But it is crucial that you realise that *your feelings are lying to you*. Not paying your adult child's speeding fines that they have accumulated themselves is NOT CRUEL. In fact you are rescuing them from their consequences, and that is the worst thing for them.

That feeling of cruelty is lying to you, and you need to use your new mindset and life coaches to over-ride it.

BELOW IS A LIST OF *INSIGHTS* OR *COACHES* for re-training your self-talk. Read through these and MEMORISE the ones that really strike a chord with you. You may change a few key words if that helps them really work for you.

Because most enabling parents are 'rescuers' by nature, they often get their worth or value from feeling needed or being approved of. There is also a lot of guilt that can happen as they consider putting on the brakes and no longer enabling. Therefore some of these insights relate to where we get approval from and the repercussions of guilt.

Repeat after me:

I'm not being cruel when I am saying 'no'.

I am not depriving them of anything; at least not of anything that they really need.

Their reaction and mood is their responsibility, not mine.

Just because I'm feeling guilty doesn't make me bad. It's an old feeling that was used to manipulate me. These new boundaries are healthy and I'm proud of them.

My feelings aren't in charge of me.

My feelings can be wrong – if they are mis-representing reality to me then it's okay to talk back to them.

My emotions in this situation are lying to me, they are reflecting past beliefs and conclusions that were wrong.

Their over-reaction or rejection says more about them than it does about me.

I am a loving person, and it's okay to put boundaries around my compassion so it's not taken advantage of.

I choose to take my worth and value back into my hands, and will no longer wait for it to be validated by others and their approval of me.

I have inherent value and worth as a human being, and I deserve to be treated well and respected.

I am trying my best as a parent and providing them with all that they 'actually need', and perhaps just passing on a few frivolities.

It's okay to leave my children to face the consequences of their own actions. Consequences are great teachers.

By setting boundaries I am protecting my empathy and stopping myself from 'burning out' and becoming resentful. Therefore I am making sure I can continue to be a helpful, loving person for years to come.

As a parent, I am doing the best that I can for my children and I have their best interests at heart.

Cruel, mean or un-kind words will no longer control me or my reactions. I own my generosity and it's okay to set limits around it.

Enabling won't buy me love.

I have to take care of myself. The more healthy and balanced I am, then the more I will be able to help others from an attitude of generosity rather than resentment.

I deserve to be treated with respect.

If my worth and value lies in others hands, then they can take it away at any time.

Guilt makes me emotionally weak, and makes me feel like I'm worthless. This is not the truth. I'm a loving, empathetic person...and these new boundaries are loving and empathetic. Guilt has no place here.

If I just focus on feeling guilty then there's no room in my life for positive change.

I don't need to 'do things for others' to feel significant or valued. I approve of myself, and I accept myself.

If they can't give me my value, then they can't take it away from me.

Memorise the insights that best apply to you. Tweak them to make them even more specific to your situation, or simplify them if that is better for you.

But whatever you do...

MEMORISE THEM!!!

If you have simply read them, liked them, and got the general idea, then that's not a bad thing. But when you hit that challenging situation you wont have anything solid to hold onto.

To train new grooves in your brain you NEED to have a few of these memorised and at your fingertips.

Learn to Say 'no'

Saying 'no' to some frivolities may bring on a sulking kid or a fit of tears, but it is something that you are doing for their future. Saying 'no' is not being cruel to them, rather it is teaching your children their boundaries. It is teaching them that not everything is attainable only by asking for it, or by throwing a tantrum; you will have to wait to achieve something or work to get it.

By saying 'no', you are actually preparing them for the real world outside their comfort zone where everyone will constantly be saying 'no'.

"Can I have two cakes this birthday, dad?"

"No, baby. One is more than enough, and we're going to have a great birthday party."

"Can I have the money for the trainers, mom?"

"No, son. Not until your old ones are used up properly."

"I need your red vintage dress, mom. Do I have to return it?"

"You can borrow it. But please take care of it and yes, of course, I will need it back. It's my dress. And if I feel like it, I may give it to you one day."

"Can I get some help with my rent and food this month? I will definitely pay you back."

"No. We'd love it if you come over for dinner as much as you want. However regarding money, you still haven't paid us back for any of our previous loans. Until a repayment scheme is started we won't be loaning you any more money."

See how that works? You are saying no, but you are also saying why, and putting boundaries around each situation. In this way you can also start to teach your adult child how they can earn your trust back.

Change your Thinking

Before you advance to change your children, it is you who needs to change your behavior. Yes, you!

I know that as a parent, it can break your heart to deny your child something, even if they are now an adult. But you cannot expect your adult children to magically become independent and confident human beings if you continue to enable them.

Change your own behavior and stop planning your children's lives for them. Stop giving constant advice on how to lead their lives. Accept within yourself that your children have grown up and that they have a life and a mind of their own.

Chapter 6 – Practical Steps For Putting Your New Thinking and Boundaries Into Action

So, you are worried that you may be enabling your growing child too much? Or, do you have a grown up son or a daughter who is still behaving like a child? Now that you are aware of the problem, it is time to do something about it.

As the name of the chapter suggests, I have compiled for you some practical steps for putting your new ideas into action. Let's go through them, shall we?

Step#1: No time like right now

Right now – this is the perfect time to start. Whether your children are in their teens, and still behaving in an irresponsible and careless manner, or whether they are old enough to start their own families, if you feel like things have gone on too far, this is the right time to start...

Or stop! Stop enabling your adult child so that they start behaving like the adult that they actually are. Stop all your pampering and your coddling and begin to treat them like the grown-ups they are.

They have grown up, they have hands and feet and a brain that works. Let them earn their own living, let them wash and clean their own shirts, let them clean their own room/house, let them cook their own dinner – and if they can't, well there's always something open 24/7.

Instead of doing everything for them that they are capable of doing for themselves, just stop!

Step#2: Stop making excuses

"But he works so hard all day and earns almost nothing. How can I not help him?"

"But she doesn't know how to cook; she has never cooked anything in her life. I have to cook for her."

"She's too young to make such a decision on her own."

"There's no way he's capable of living on his own. What would he eat? What would he wear?"

"I'm just helping him get through the week; it's only until he gets a new job."

"She just wants to take a break before she looks for a job... a long break!"

"She just broke up with someone serious. I need to look after her for some time."

"He's not an addict. He just drinks a few beers when he's depressed. I would have never supported him if he was an addict."

"Of course she doesn't have a shopping disorder! She just likes fancy clothes too much and can't control herself sometimes."

"She's not an alcoholic! Alcoholics are dirty, smelly and dumb, and don't have homes or jobs. She's just a social drinker!"

Sounds familiar? No matter whether the child is 30 or 80, parents are always making excuses for them. Well, it's time.

Stop making excuses. Period.

There are no 'if's or but's' about it. Your children are adults and they should behave and act like adults. If they are not earning much, that's okay, they can survive on that (as millions of other people do), as they work their way up. Ask them to get cooking lessons, why endlessly cook for them?

Step#3: Stop fixing their lives

We all have time when we get into trouble in life... and then we get ourselves out of it. Most of the time it is we alone who have to face the world and get our lives back on track. Of course, most of us have people in our lives that will help us when we need it, but at the end of the day we face the consequences for our actions and have to deal with our issues ourselves. However this is how we learn, and this is how we get the strength to move on in life.

If every time your children get into trouble you intervene to fix the problem, then they will miss out on this valuable lesson in life. So your son broke someone's window while playing? Send him to the neighbor's house to say sorry and let him figure out a way to pay for the damage. Don't apologize for him and don't offer to pay up; instead, send him to work off his debt if he cannot pay with his pocket money.

Your grownup son has recently developed a liking for expensive gadgets? And now he's maxed out his credit card? Oh, and his salary is gone too? Too bad! But don't worry, he'll figure something out. He'll get a loan from his office, or work out a way to pay it off gradually. He needs to be the one to solve this, not you! You didn't ask him to buy the new iPad, why should you pay his credit card bills?

Step#4: Let them make their own decisions

As a parent, it certainly is your job to guide and advise them, but as your children grow up, they should be allowed to make their own decisions, and their own mistakes.

Whether it is the decision of which college to apply for, or whether to take a loan to buy a car, let them take the risks and evaluate the options. Share your opinions and give your thoughts on the matter, but don't force it on them.

Parents like to be in control. Raising a child from its first day in this world gets parents into the habit of making every decision for them; what they eat, what they wear, what they think and what they feel. It is only natural. But when the child has grown up into an adult, it is time to give the control of their lives over to them.

Watch them make their own decisions. If they fail or make a mistake, pick them up, set them straight, and then watch them have another go at the problem.

Step#5: Know the difference between 'helping' and 'enabling'

There is a difference between helping your child and enabling your child that is easy to miss. Introducing your daughter to a friend who might have a job for her is helping her; forcing your friend to give her a job that she's not capable of would be enabling her. Helping with rent money for two months when your son is between jobs is helping; continuously paying his expenses because your son can't seem to hold on to a job, or doesn't bother looking for a job, is enabling him.

You should always help your child, of course; but it is not right that you should continually rescue them, or be the 'backup guy' in every situation.

Step#6: Stop nitpicking

Nitpicking is not a healthy approach to parenting. Avoid nitpicking at all costs if you want to empower, not enable, your children. If you are constantly finding faults with your children, they will grow up knowing that they cannot do anything right. Constant nitpicking will lower their self-esteem and confidence in venturing out into the big wide world.

Stop criticizing the state of your daughter's kitchen. If she wants to live like a pig, let her. Don't harass your son constantly about his next promotion or raise. When he is ready, he will reach that goal too. Whatever your children are doing, and wherever they are in their lives, should be enough for you to be proud of them.

Step#7: Stop feeling guilty

Learn to say no to all the "Mom, can you please do the laundry?" and "Dad, I need to borrow a few dollars, I'm going out with my friends". And when the unexpected 'no' is followed by "But, mom!" and "You're my father, you have to take care of me!", stop feeling guilty about it.

This is just your children's technique to manipulate you into doing what they need. If you are adamant on your decision not to help them on jobs that they should be doing themselves, they will slowly get the message.

Step#8: Keep your lives separate

Your adult children, whether they are living with you, or whether they are constantly keeping you at their beck and call, need to come to terms with the fact that you have a separate life from them. It is not your only aim in life to be forever present when they need you. They need to understand that you do not belong to them, and that you are not their personal agony aunt, their personal housekeeper, or their personal butler.

Your children need to respect the fact that you have plans in your life that are separate from them, and that you need privacy and space just like any other normal person does.

Make them understand that you have almost finished your obligation as their parents; that they have grown up enough to lead their own lives, leaving you to lead your own life. It is time that you go your separate ways in life.

You are going to the Opera with your partner this evening and you will not change your plans when they call you out of the blue to baby-sit for the children. Yes, you would love to see your grandchildren and of course you would want to help them out, but they should have been considerate enough to ask ahead of time without assuming that you will put your entire life on hold for them. Let them know that you can't help because you have plans, but please to call ahead the next time they need babysitting help, because YOU HAVE A LIFE TOO!

Step#9: Be very strict about their finances

One common way that we enable children is by helping them financially. While it is perfectly okay to occasionally give them an expensive present or help them out of a tough spot, these adult children learn very quickly to manipulate their parents regarding money.

- Do not pay off your children's debts.

- Do not lend them money if they fail to return it more than once.

- Do not pay for mortgages or sign the co-mortgage for a house when you know they will never be able to pay it off.

- God forbid, if they end up in jail, do not bail them out repeatedly.

- Do not pay for their drinks or for partying.

- Do not help out with rent money when they are earning but

still not paying for rent and other necessities.

- Do not pay for groceries/food, or invite them over constantly, because they declare that they have no money to spend on food even though they are employed. Chances are, they're wasting their money on something frivolous.

- Don't pay for maxed-out or overdrawn credit cards when it is apparent that they are using the money for shopping and partying.

- Do not lend them money if you suspect they may be using it to buy drugs or alcohol.

In other words, Mom and Dad must stop being the banks once children have grown up. Do not end up being your son or your daughter's backup plan, or their 'Get Out Of Jail Free' card.

"Lend me some money, mom. I bought a new dress this month and now I am out of cash. I'll pay you back this time, I swear!"

"Can you lend me a few bucks, dad? A couple of us guys are planning to go hiking this month, and you know I give Mandy all my salary for the groceries."

"Help me out this time, dad! I swear it was an accident. I wasn't drinking, and it was the other driver's fault, trust me!"

Beware of these situations. They're an easy target for gullible parents to become overly sympathetic.

Step#10: Do not do their chores

Whether your adult child is living with you in your home, or whether they have separate accommodations nearby, you should definitely not be doing their chores. If your grownup children have decided to live with you, they should take part in the chores around the house and look after themselves.

Do not do their laundry, do not clean their rooms, require them to cook dinner at least twice a week, and give them cleaning chores around the house. If they are working, then ensure that they pay for board or for groceries. By no means should you struggle to make ends meet when your adult child is living with you, but not contributing to the expenses.

Many times parents step over the boundary and begin to enable. It is their instinct and it's in their nature to be protective of their children and to shelter them from the rest of the world. But it is when parents misjudge the fine line between *helping* and *enabling* that they put their children at the risk of not growing up.

Use the insights in the previous chapter to re-train your thinking and your self-talk. *Memorise, memorise, memorise!!*

Repeatedly read the list of boundaries in Chapter six, and use them create your new boundaries.

Use your fresh perspective to communicate your new stance with dignified assertiveness.

Be calm, strong, and hold to your new boundaries!!!

Remember, you are still a loving, empathetic and helpful person. By 'sticking to your guns', and enforcing these boundaries, you are actually doing the most loving thing you can.

Believe that. This is the most loving and caring action you can take, both for yourself and for your adult child.

Conclusion

I hope this book was able to help you to feel in control of your life again, as you challenge your mis-beliefs about enabling. I hope you feel progressively more empowered as you use your healthy boundaries to re-define your relationships. It will take time and consistency, but be gentle on yourself when you make a mistake, and enjoy your journey towards feeling happier and freer as you stop rescuing!

The next step is to consistently put your new boundaries and strategies in place with dignified assertiveness. There are a lot of other great resources out there that will also help. If you are interested in the strategies of Cognitive Behavioural Therapy, then there are some great books that go into it in more depth that could be beneficial.

Also, use your support network! You probably have more people there ready to support you than you realise. Family and friends can be our greatest resource, and we often forget this as we think we need to 'do it on our own'. Accept help from the people who love you as you go on this journey.

Thank you and good luck!

Melody Devonish

References

Beck, A. T. (1976). *Cognitive Therapy and the Emotional Disorders*. The Penguin Group. New York, United States.

Bourne, E. J. PH.D. (2005). *The Anxiety & Phobia Workbook. Fourth Edition*. New Harbinger Publications, Inc. CA, United States

Edelman, S. Phd. (2006). *Change Your Thinking. Second Edition.* ABC Books, Australia

Froggatt, W. (2003). *Fearless*. HarperCollins Publishers, New Zealand

Willson, R. & Branch, R. (2006) *Cognitive Behavioural Therapy for Dummies*. John Wiley & Sons Ltd. England

Verrier, N. N. (2010). *Coming Home To Self*. British Association for Adoption and Fostering. England

Websites:

http://destructivecycles.blogspot.co.nz/2009/10/reach-for-wise-mind.html

http://yorindawanner.com/making-changes-and-the-limbic-lag/

Made in the USA
Lexington, KY
14 January 2019